AF576821

Perfection Learning®

Dedication

To Sue Thies

About the Author

Bonnie Highsmith Taylor is a native Oregonian. She loves camping in the Oregon mountains and watching birds and other wildlife. Writing is Ms. Taylor's first love. But she also enjoys going to plays and concerts, collecting antique dolls, and listening to good music.

Image Credits: Art Today pp. 5, 6, 7, 9 (bottom), 11, 12 (bottom), 19, 20 (bottom), 21 (middle), 25, 26 (bottom), 27, 28, 29, 30, 31, 32, 33, 34 (top), 35 (top), 36 (bottom), 40, 46, 47, 51, 53; Corbis/Bettmann pp. 36 (top), 38 (top), 41, 44 (top), 50, 52, 57, 59 (bottom), 61 (bottom); Library of Congress pp. 12 (top), 15, 16, 18, 21 (top and bottom), 22, 23, 24, 34 (bottom), 35 (second, third, bottom), 38 (bottom), 39, 42, 43 (bottom), 44 (bottom), 49, 59 (top), 60 (top); Maria Mitchell Association pp. 4, 9 (top), 10; National Archives pp. 26 (top), 43 (top), 44 (middle), 45, 54, 55, 56, 60 (bottom), 61 (top); National Park Service pp. 14 (bottom), 20 (top); New Rochelle School of Nursing pp. 37, 38 (bottom); New York Public Library p. 14 (top)

Printed in the United States of America. For information, contact
Perfection Learning® Corporation, 1000 North Second Avenue,
P.O. Box 500, Logan, Iowa 51546-0500.
Phone: 1-800-831-4190 • Fax: 1-712-644-2392
Paperback ISBN 0-7891-5045-x
Cover Craft® ISBN 0-7807-9019-7

Table of Contents

Maria Mitchell

Chapter 1

Maria Mitchell

First American Woman Astronomer

"Why does Jupiter have four moons, Father?" asked Maria. "The earth doesn't have that many."

William Mitchell lowered his newspaper. He looked at his small daughter. "I am not sure, Maria. Maybe because it is such a large planet. Much larger than our Earth."

Maria's older sister, Sally, was sewing by the fire. Eleven-year-old Andrew bent over his books at the table. Little Ann and Willie were already asleep in their trundle beds. Mrs. Mitchell rocked the cradle to quiet baby Francis.

"Who named the Big Dipper and the Little Dipper, Father?" questioned Maria. She hung over Mr. Mitchell's shoulder.

"Perhaps American Indians, long ago," Father replied. "People have studied the skies since the beginning of time."

"The dippers are our star calendar, aren't they, Father?"

"And our star clock too," Mr. Mitchell answered.

"Must thee ask so many questions?" Mrs. Mitchell scolded Maria.

"But, Mother. I need to know these things to become an **astronomer."**

"Thee will not be an astronomer," said Mother. "Girls cannot be astronomers."

"Why not?"

"It is not fitting for a girl," Mrs. Mitchell explained. "Especially for a Quaker girl. Thee must learn to sew, cook, and keep a clean house." She pulled a coverlet over the sleeping baby. "Thy brother Andrew will be an astronomer. Like thy father. Not thee."

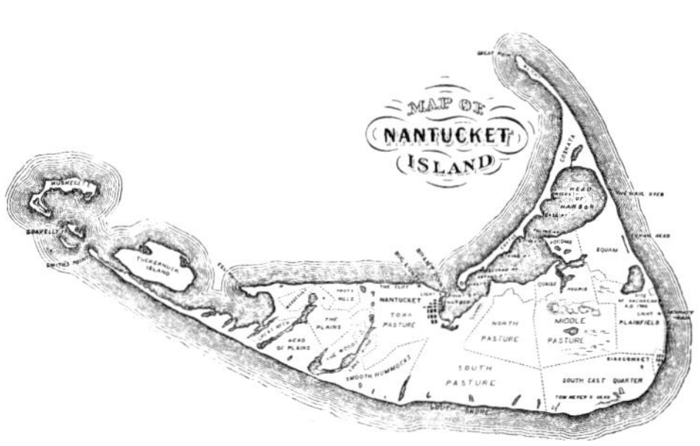

But Andrew did not want to be an astronomer. He was like most boys who lived on Nantucket Island. He wanted to go to sea. He wanted to be a whaler.

Most evenings, all the Mitchell children loved to climb the stairs to the walk on the roof. That's when Father swept the sky with his telescope.

But Maria loved it most of all. She loved looking at the stars and learning their names. She loved learning how to adjust the telescope and how to use the **sextant** and **chronometer.**

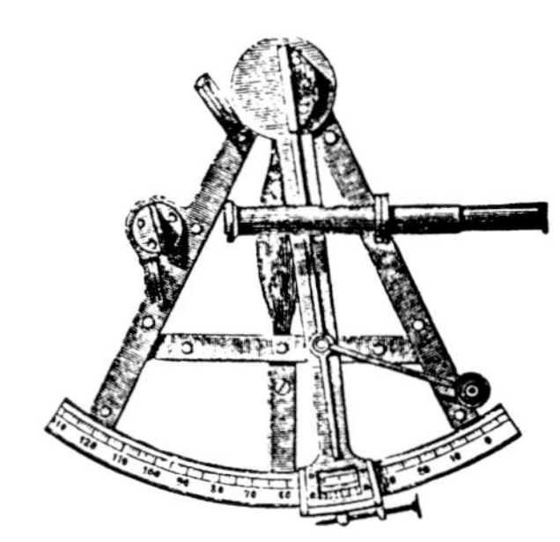

Father had told her, "The chronometer is a sailor's clock. Sailors use the chronometer and the sextant to tell where they are at sea."

"Why is the chronometer inside a box, Father?" Maria had asked.

"There are rings inside the box," said Mr. Mitchell. "The rings keep the chronometer level no matter how much the ship rocks."

Every day, Maria learned more about astronomy from her father. And at night before she fell asleep, she whispered into her pillow, "I will be an astronomer! I *will!*"

Maria was born in 1818. She was the second daughter and third child in a family that would reach ten. She grew up in a strict Quaker household.

Maria and her siblings were not allowed to attend circuses, fairs, or minstrel shows that came to town. Their clothes were practical and unadorned. Their food was nutritious but plain.

One of the most exciting experiences of Maria's young life was when she saw an **eclipse** of the sun.

"It will not be a total eclipse," Father explained. "It will be what is called an *annular eclipse.* A thin circle of sunlight will show all around the moon as it covers the sun."

"But what if it's foggy or cloudy?" said Maria.

Father smiled. "Thee frets too much. Now help thy sister smoke some glass to look through."

Sally lit candles. Then she and Maria smoked a piece of glass for each member of the family.

Maria could hardly sleep the night before the eclipse was to take place. "Oh please, God," she prayed, "let it be a clear day."

The sky was gray and cloudy when the family awoke in the morning. Sally and Maria sniffled and blinked back tears. The smaller children whimpered. Even Andrew looked as though he wanted to cry.

"Be patient," Mr. Mitchell said. "The eclipse is not to start until nearly noon."

Then a few minutes before noon, the clouds rolled away.

Maria jumped for joy as she yelled, "They're gone! The clouds are gone!"

"Control thyself, child," scolded Mother. "Such unladylike conduct."

For the next three hours, Maria held the smoked glass before her eyes. She watched the miracle. When the sun was almost completely covered, stars appeared in the sky.

Maria had a chance to prove how much she had learned from her father when she was only 12. Ship captains from all around Nantucket Island came to William Mitchell. He would set chronometers for them.

One day, Father was away. Captain Chadwick called at the Mitchell house. When he heard that William would not be back for several days, he was very upset. "My ship is sailing tomorrow, and my chronometer needs correcting. What will I do?"

"I can do it, Captain Chadwick," Maria spoke up.

"Thee knows thee cannot," Mother said.

"But, Mother. I have watched Father many times. I have even helped him."

The old captain studied the girl for a moment.

"Well, I certainly can't do it!" the captain exclaimed. "And I know of no one else on the island who can." He looked from the box in his hand to Maria. "I'll take a chance," he said at last.

Maria could hardly wait for dark. When it finally came, she took her father's sextant, the whale-oil lamp, and the captain's chronometer outside. She spent most of the night rating the instrument.

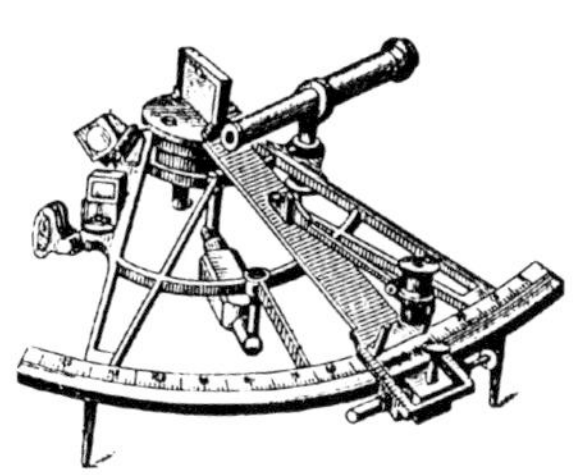

She pointed the telescope on the sextant at a star. She measured the height of the star. Then she checked the time on the chronometer and wrote it down. She aimed at another star and repeated the process.

Finally, Maria was sure she had rated the instrument correctly. She climbed upstairs and went to bed.

By the end of the week, it was all over the island. William Mitchell's daughter had done as good a job as her father.

When Maria was only 17, she started her own school. She placed an ad in the paper.

> **S C H O O L**
>
> MARIA MITCHELL PROPOSES TO OPEN A SCHOOL FOR GIRLS ON THE FIRST OF NEXT MONTH AT THE FRANKLIN SCHOOL HOUSE. INSTRUCTION WILL BE GIVEN IN READING, SPELLING, GEOGRAPHY, GRAMMAR, HISTORY, NATURAL PHILOSOPHY, ARITHMETIC, GEOMETRY, AND ALGEBRA. TERMS $3 PER QUARTER. NONE ADMITTED UNDER SIX YEARS OF AGE.

Maria enjoyed teaching. But she was uneasy about her own lack of education. There was so much she wanted to know. More than anything, she wanted to go to college. But how could a girl go to college? College was for boys.

She had heard of a school in Ohio that admitted girls. But there were only a few courses girls could take.

After a year of teaching, Maria went to work as a librarian at the Nantucket Atheneum. There, she was able to further her education on her own. She read every book on astronomy.

All of Maria's brothers and sisters married. But she stayed single.

When she was about 16, she became very close to Ebenezer Mason. He shared her interest in astronomy. Shortly after he graduated from Yale, he died from a lung disease.

Ten years later, Maria met George Bond. He was the son of her father's astronomer friend. Maria did love him. But she refused to marry him because of their ages. She was seven years older.

October 1, 1847, became an important date in Maria's life. She was sweeping the skies all alone one evening. It was a clear, beautiful night—an astronomer's night!

Usually Father was with her. But that night, he had guests.

It was cold on the roof. Even so, Maria would not go in when the skies were this bright and clear.

She swept the telescope across a wide area. Suddenly her hands froze. Just above the North Star, she saw a small, hazy spot. It had not been there before. That she was sure of. She studied it for a long time.

It was moving! It was a comet! She knew it had to be.

She nearly fell as she rushed down the stairs. From the doorway, she motioned to Father. He followed her back to the roof.

Mr. Mitchell adjusted the telescope to his eye.

"Maria," he gasped. "It is a comet! You have discovered a comet!"

Later that evening, he made a recording in his notebook.

> *10m. 1, 1847. This evening at half past ten Maria discovered a telescopic comet five degrees above Polaris. Persuaded that no* ***nebula*** *could occupy that position unnoticed, it scarcely needed the evidence of motion to give it the character of a comet.*

William Mitchell wasted no time in writing the news of the discovery to an astronomer friend. But because of a bad storm at sea, the mail was held up for three days.

The friend, on receiving the letter, notified the proper authorities of Maria's find. In the next few days, three other reports of the comet were made. But the date on Mr. Mitchell's letter proved that Maria's sighting was the first. The comet was named the Maria Mitchell Comet.

For her discovery, Maria was awarded a gold medal by the King of Denmark. One side of the medal was inscribed with her name and the date of the sighting. On the other side was the inscription "Not in vain do we watch the setting and rising of the stars."

This was only one of the many honors that Maria Mitchell received in her lifetime. In 1848, she was the first woman admitted to the American Academy of Arts and Sciences. She received a

Maria Mitchell

medal of merit from the Republic of San Marino. She was given a Diploma of Honor for her notes on the satellites of Saturn and Jupiter.

For five years, she did observations for the *National Almanac.*

In 1865, a new school for women opened in Poughkeepsie, New York. It was Vassar Female College. (In 1867, feminist Sarah J. Hale succeeded in getting the word *female* deleted from the name.)

Though Maria had never been to college herself, she was a professor of astronomy at the school from its opening until 1888.

The new school had very strict rules.

- A YOUNG LADY MUST NOT CROSS HER FEET IN THE PARLOR.
- SHE MUST NOT SIT SIDEWAYS ON A CHAIR.
- SHE MUST NOT SHOW HER ANKLES.
- SHE MUST NOT MAKE A HORSESHOE WHEN BITING INTO A PIECE OF BREAD.
- SHE MUST NOT LEAVE HER ROOM AFTER TEN O'CLOCK.

Maria's pupils were often guilty of breaking the last rule.

Maria tried to reason with her superiors. "How am I to teach astronomy in the middle of the day when there are no moon and stars?"

Maria was nearly 70 years old when she retired. She died on June 28, 1889, at the age of 71.

The house in Nantucket where she was born became the Maria Mitchell Museum.

In a public library in Boston, a metal band on the wall bears the names of famous astronomers. Along with Galileo and Newton, William Herschel, and Mary Somerville is the name of Maria Mitchell.

Harriet Tubman

Conductor of Freedom

Harriet Tubman once received a letter and an invitation to a birthday celebration from Queen Victoria. She was an honored guest in the home of poet and essayist Ralph Waldo Emerson.

Queen Victoria

Harriet was a close friend of Louisa May Alcott's family. She spoke on platforms with Susan B. Anthony and Elizabeth Cady Stanton. During the Civil War, she advised and worked hand in hand with noted Union officers.

* * *

Harriet was born around 1820. She lived in a crude cabin with a dirt floor and no windows. She was a nobody—a slave child.

By the time she was six years old, she was a servant in her master's house. Her jobs were to help peel potatoes and carry water from the well. She scrubbed the floors on her hands and knees. And she had to keep the baby happy. Even though it was all she could do to lift him.

As a slave, Harriet had no rights. Her master or mistress could work her from sunrise to sunset. They could whip her as they wished. If the baby cried, she was whipped.

"I've told you and told you," her mistress panted between blows of the leather strap. "Never let the baby cry."

"But, Missus. I couldn't make him stop."

Again, the whip lashed across her back.

"And what have I told you?" her mistress yelled. "Don't talk back!"

Harriet's parents, brothers, and sisters were all slaves on a tobacco plantation near the village of Bucktown, Maryland. Life was bad. There was always the fear of being sold down South to the cotton planters.

Sometimes Ma would try to console her children. She'd say, "We got it good alongside those cotton slaves down South."

Harriet wasn't very old when she learned that the South was bad. The North was good. Old Ned had said so. And he ought to know.

Old Ned had been born on the slave ship that brought his people from Africa to America. He was the oldest person on the plantation.

Young field slave

"Up North, a Negro can be free," he said. "Nobody can own slaves."

He told all the other slaves Bible stories and taught them songs. Harriet learned about the children of Israel who had been held in Egypt by the Pharaoh. She'd raise her voice and sing loudly the songs Ned taught.

Go down, Moses,
Way down in Egypt's land.
Tell ol' Pharaoh,
Let my people go.

One night, two slaves disappeared from a neighboring plantation. It was then that Harriet first learned about the Underground Railroad.

"It's not a real train," Old Ned explained. "Its conductors are people who are against slavery. They hide slaves in their homes. When it is safe, the slaves move to the next station. They finally get North to the free states. There they find jobs and homes."

From then on, Harriet could think of nothing else. One day she would go North and be free.

Harriet was 15. She was sent to a country store on an errand. An **overseer** from a plantation nearby came in with a slave.

"You wait in the corner, Jim," the overseer said. "Soon as I get this order filled, you can tote it home."

Suddenly, Jim bolted for the open door.

"Get back here, you black devil!" roared the overseer. He looked at Harriet and cried, "Grab him, girl! Grab him."

But Harriet jumped in front of the white man. She stretched out her arms. Over her shoulders, she could see Jim running into the woods.

In a rage, the overseer grabbed a heavy weight off the counter. He threw it at Harriet. It hit her on the side of the head.

For a long time after that, Harriet was unconscious. She was not expected to live. For the rest of her life, she had a deep dent in her head. She suffered from sleeping spells. She could fall asleep while hoeing in the field or carrying a bucket of water from the well.

Harriet was 24 years old when she married John Tubman, a free Negro. John was quite content with his life. He tried to discourage Harriet when she talked of riding the Underground Railroad to freedom.

It didn't bother John that he was not allowed to own land, vote, carry a gun, attend a church that had a black minister, or even own a dog. He just liked being called "free."

Slaves escaping

The time came for Harriet to run away. She kept it a secret from her husband.

Harriet had heard about the white people who were called *Quakers*. She knew that they hated slavery. They even helped Negroes escape up North.

It was through a Quaker family who lived in Bucktown that Harriet got the information she needed. They told her the route to freedom.

"Just follow the Choptank River. Go to where it begins at the border between Maryland and Delaware. Then take the road to Camden. Go northeast until you come to a clapboard house with green shutters."

Harriet's brothers, William, Robert, and Benjamin, set out with her. But in a short time, they decided the risks were too great.

"We'll never make it, sister," said William. "They'll catch us. Things will be worse than ever."

Benjamin pleaded, "Come back with us. Please."

But Harriet went on alone. For two weeks, she trudged through woods, meadows, and thickets. Sometimes she waded in water and mud.

Most of the time, she traveled at night. But she kept going. Often she sang silently, "I'm bound for the promised land."

At last the door of the clapboard house opened. A kind voice said, "Come in, friend. Thee are welcome." Harriet breathed a sigh of joy.

But Harriet was not completely satisfied. Not when so many of her family and friends were still in bondage. And as wonderful as it was to be free, Harriet was lonely. She had to go back to set them free.

Harriet began her life as "Moses."

She crossed into enemy territory 19 times. She succeeded in leading over 300 slaves to freedom. The reward for her capture eventually reached $40,000. In spite of the danger, she never gave up.

The slave owners were furious. "Something must be done about that thieving black wench," they ranted. "She ought to be strung up."

In 1850, the Fugitive Slave Law was passed. Slaves were no longer safe in any of the states. The new law denied runaway slaves the right to a trial if caught. Anyone found aiding a slave could be fined and imprisoned.

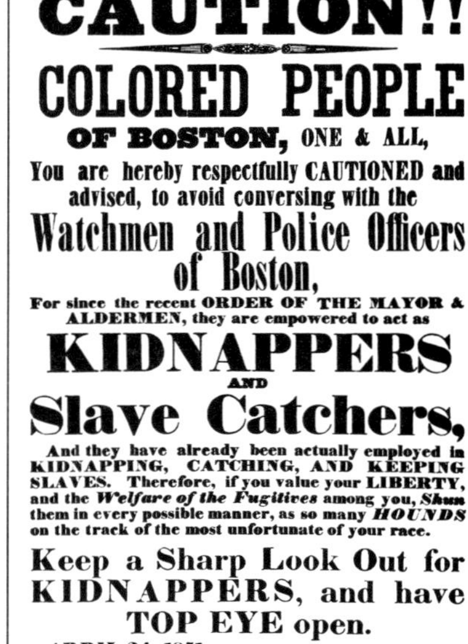

There were nearly 50,000 Negroes living in the North at the time. Most of them were escaped slaves.

Once more, they had to flee to freedom. This time they went to Canada where they were welcome.

The new law made Harriet's job a little more difficult. The Underground Railroad would have to run a little farther north. But it would not stop.

Harriet's fame grew. She was talked about in every town from Canada to the Gulf of Mexico.

"What a daring woman," they said. "She must have magical powers!"

"She's another Moses," some stated. "She's freeing her people single-handed."

Blacks claimed she was ten feet tall! She could see in the dark! She could jump over rivers and mountains too.

Harriet Tubman laughed at these claims. But she did say, "As a conductor of the Underground Railroad, I can say what most conductors can't. I never ran my train off the track. And I never lost a passenger."

❈ ❈ ❈

When the Civil War began in 1861, Harriet volunteered as a nurse, cook, and laundress to help the Union. She and other volunteer escaped slaves followed the army from camp to camp.

At the request of General Hunter, Harriet formed a group of scouts to go ahead of the troops. They looked for rebel outposts.

"It's very dangerous, Harriet," the general said. "I'll understand if you refuse."

"I was born to danger, sir," Harriet replied.

Harriet Tubman

Because of Harriet and her black scouts, many successful raids were made.

Harriet had discovered one of the main Confederate camps at Green Pond. It was not far from the Combahee River. There were big plantations with hundreds of slaves on both sides of the river.

"We should surprise them in the middle of the night," Harriet explained to Colonel James Montgomery. "Then we could wipe out their supplies."

"But we'd have to take boats up the river in the dark," the colonel reasoned. "We don't know the river. There are sure to be torpedoes in the water. It's not safe."

"My scouts know the river. And we know where the explosives are. We can steer around them easily."

At last, Colonel Montgomery was convinced. He put Harriet in charge of 300 black soldiers.

Three Union gunboats left St. Helena Sound at midnight. The mission was a big success. They captured the Confederate camp and destroyed the supplies. They also freed 800 slaves from plantations and took them back to the army base.

After the war, Harriet returned to Auburn, New York. There she cared for her aged parents and continued working for her people.

In 1869, Sarah Hopkins Bradford wrote a biography of Harriet, *Scenes in the Life of Harriet Tubman.* Harriet received $1,200 of the proceeds. She used that and her government pension money to manage an old folks home for Negroes. She called it the John Brown Home.

She continued working for her people until she died on March 10, 1913. She was given a military funeral.

In 1914, a bronze plaque in her memory was hung on the wall of the Cayuga County Courthouse.

In Memory of Harriet Tubman
Born a slave in Maryland about 1821
Died in Auburn, N.Y., March 10, 1913
Called the "Moses" of her people,
During the Civil War, with rare
Courage, she led over three hundred
Negroes up from slavery to freedom
And rendered invaluable service
As nurse and spy.
With implicit trust in God
She braved every danger and
Overcame every obstacle, [yet]
She possessed extraordinary
Foresight and judgment so that
She truthfully said—
"On my Underground Railroad
I never ran my train off the track
And I never lost a passenger."
THIS TABLET IS ERECTED
BY THE CITIZENS OF AUBURN

Chapter 3

Susan B. Anthony

"The Dear Old Liberator"

Little did Mr. and Mrs. Anthony know what a difference their new baby daughter would make in the world someday. She was born on February 15, 1820. They named her Susan Brownell.

"A rather plain-looking baby," said Daniel Anthony. "But at least she's healthy."

"She's beautiful," insisted Lucy Anthony. "She has a nice little face. Full of character and—"

The infant let forth a wail that rang through the house.

"Determination," laughed Susan's father.

How right he was.

Susan's determination was strong. And throughout her life it never died.

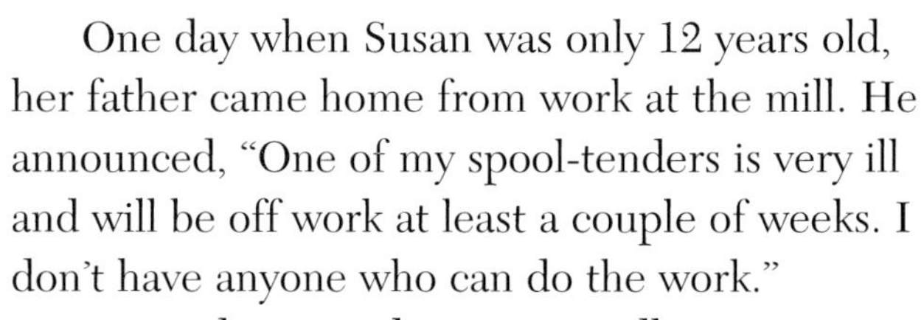

One day when Susan was only 12 years old, her father came home from work at the mill. He announced, "One of my spool-tenders is very ill and will be off work at least a couple of weeks. I don't have anyone who can do the work."

"I can do it," said Susan proudly.

"Hush, Susan," Mrs. Anthony scolded. "You're only a child."

"But, Mama. Papa has taken me to the mill many times. I've watched the spoolers wind the thread," explained Susan. "I know I can do it."

Mr. Anthony studied his daughter for a moment. Then he said, "I believe she can, Lucy. I just believe she can."

For the next two weeks, Susan filled in for the absent spool-tender and earned three dollars. It was her first job.

When Susan was 15, her father opened a school in their home. She became the teacher.

Susan's father enrolled her in a Quaker boarding school in Philadelphia when she was 17. Her older sister, Guelma, also attended the school.

The school was 300 miles from their home in Battenville, New York. The trip took nearly a week. So Mr. Anthony went with his daughters.

After her father left, Susan was homesick. She could hardly bear it. In her diary she wrote, "Oh, what pangs were felt. It seemed impossible for me to part with him."

However, six months later, Susan was back home with her family. It was 1838. The United States was in a financial depression.

Mr. Anthony had come to the school for the girls. "I've lost everything," Mr. Anthony had told his daughters. "My business is gone. I've lost the house. The furniture. Everything!"

Even Mrs. Anthony's personal belongings were taken to pay his debts. Susan was very angry. But by law, a wife's property belonged to her husband.

The family moved to Center Falls, New York. Mr. Anthony owned another small cotton mill there. The mill had never been successful. It was also heavily in debt. But he decided to give it another try.

Susan and her sisters, Guelma and Hannah, along with 14-year-old Daniel, helped out all they could. There were also two younger children, Mary and Merritt.

Susan worked as a teacher. She gave the family most of her wages.

Over the years, Susan received several proposals of marriage. She turned them down. She resented most men's attitudes toward women.

Susan's brother-in-law once said, "I'd rather see a woman bake a good pie than solve the most difficult problem in algebra." Susan retorted, "There's no reason why she can't do both."

Mr. Anthony worked hard at the mill. But he could not make a successful living.

Anthony Rochester home

In 1845, Mr. Anthony borrowed money from his wife's brother to buy a farm in Rochester, New York. He moved his family there. Guelma and Hannah were now married. They remained in Center Falls. Young Daniel had a job. So he stayed too.

❈ ❈ ❈

When Susan was 26, she was appointed headmistress at Canajoharie Academy in upstate New York. Her salary was the most a woman could make as a teacher. A man could earn at least twice as much for the same job.

After three years at the academy, Susan grew tired of teaching. She went back home. And for a time, she managed her father's farm. Her father went into the insurance business.

Susan had long been interested in the antislavery movement as well as the **temperance** issue. And she strongly believed in rights for women. That included the right to vote.

Susan attended antislavery and temperance meetings. She eventually joined the Daughters of Temperance organization.

In 1849, Susan B. Anthony made her first public speech before an audience of 200. It was a great success. From that moment on, she fought against oppression in all forms. She knew she was born to be a leader.

Elizabeth Cady Stanton

For some time, Susan had heard about Elizabeth Cady Stanton. Mrs. Stanton also supported women's rights.

In May 1851, Susan went to an antislavery meeting in Seneca Falls, New York. It was there that she finally met Mrs. Stanton in person.

"How wonderful to meet you at last," she said.

"It is wonderful to meet you too," answered Elizabeth. "It seems we have a great deal in common."

It was the beginning of a long and close friendship. Through Elizabeth Stanton, Susan met other women's rights advocates.

Among these were Horace Greeley, editor of the *New York Tribune,* and Lucy Stone. Both did much to further the women's rights movement.

Lucy Stone

Horace Greeley later changed his views. He decided that what a woman needed was not the right to vote but a "wickerwork cradle and a dimple-cheeked baby."

Horace Greeley

For many years, Susan Anthony and Elizabeth Stanton fought for women's rights. Elizabeth was a fine writer. She wrote many letters, petitions, and speeches. But she had a large family. So Susan handled most of the speaking tours.

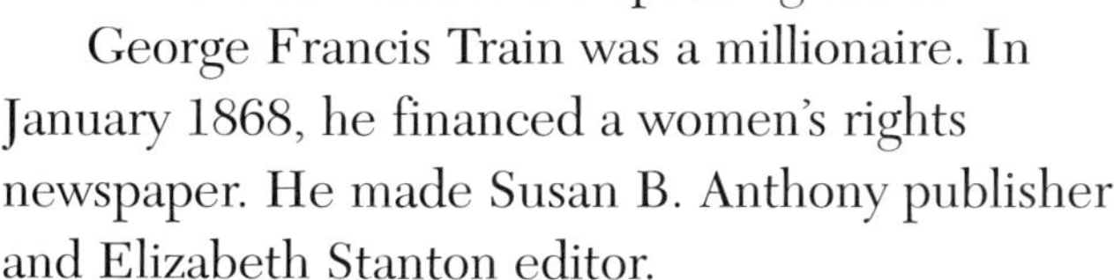

George Francis Train was a millionaire. In January 1868, he financed a women's rights newspaper. He made Susan B. Anthony publisher and Elizabeth Stanton editor.

The weekly paper was called *The Revolution.* Its motto was "Men, their rights, and nothing more. Women, their rights, and nothing less."

In Susan's diary dated January 31, 1867, she wrote, "The year goes out, and never did one depart that had been so filled with earnest and effective work! Nine thousand votes for women in Kansas, and a newspaper started. *The Revolution* is going to be work, work, and more work. The old out and the new in!"

On June 17, 1873, Susan B. Anthony went on trial for voting illegally. Susan, her sisters, and several other women had marched into the eighth precinct in Rochester, New York. They demanded to be registered.

"Registered for what?" asked the man at the desk.

"To vote," answered Susan.

"Are you crazy?" exclaimed the clerk. "Women can't vote!"

"The Fourteenth Amendment gives me the same right to vote as you," declared Susan.

She took a paper from her purse. Then she unfolded it and read, "All persons born or naturalized in the United States are citizens."

Susan B. Anthony

Susan shook her finger at the man. "Would you deny a citizen of the United States the right to register to vote?"

"But-but-" the man stammered. "You are a woman."

"And where in the constitution does it make mention of the sex of the citizen, sir?"

The man was at a loss for words. After an hour of arguing back and forth, the women were allowed to register. On election day, they cast their votes.

A United States marshal arrested Susan at her home two weeks later.

The crowded courtroom was hot and stuffy. People had come from miles around. The spectators included lawyers and reporters. Even former president Millard Fillmore was there.

Judge Ward Hunt was well known for his antifeminist views. Susan sat with her attorney as the judge took the bench. The all-male jury seated themselves in the jury box. Henry Seldon, Susan's lawyer, made a very powerful speech. The district attorney's argument followed.

Then everyone in the courtroom was surprised. Judge Hunt turned to the jury and said, "Miss Anthony was in violation of the law when she cast her vote. I direct you to find her guilty."

Mr. Seldon was on his feet. "Your Honor, I ask that you poll the jury."

The twelve men in the jury box were dazed.

"No!" snapped the judge. He waved a hand in the air. "Gentlemen of the jury, you are excused."

Susan was to be sentenced the next day. Before the sentencing, the judge asked, "Have you anything to say?"

"Yes, Your Honor. I have many things to say," she answered. "You have trampled underfoot every vital principle of our government. My natural rights, my civil rights, my political rights, my judicial rights are all alike ignored."

"That will do," the judge interrupted.

But Susan continued. "You have denied me the right to a trial by jury."

"I order you to sit down and be silent. Your sentence is a fine in the amount of one hundred dollars and court costs."

Susan B. Anthony

Susan B. Anthony looked the judge directly in the eye. She stated, "Your Honor, I shall never pay a dollar of your unjust penalty."

And she never did.

Susan continued to crusade for women's rights until the very end. She and Mrs. Stanton wrote a book, *History of Woman Suffrage.* It was published in May 1881. The book was well received by the public. *The Chicago News* called it "an important literary occurrence" and said it was a "remarkable event in the history of civilization."

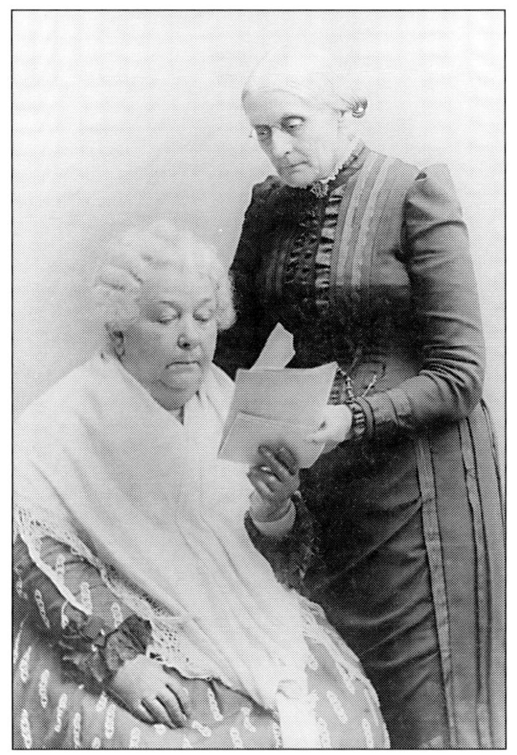

Elizabeth Cady Stanton and Susan B. Anthony

Dorothy Dix, a journalist, once wrote about Susan.

> It was my good fortune to once stand beside the dear old liberator before a distinguished audience. They cheered until they were hoarse. They threw roses until the frail figure stood almost knee-deep in flowers.
>
> When they had gone, she said with a smile trembling between a laugh and a tear, "Time brings changes. Right here where they pelt me with roses, I have been pelted with rotten eggs for saying the same thing I said tonight."

The "dear old liberator" died in Rochester, New York, on May 13, 1906, at the age of 86.

One hundred years after her birth, her lifelong dream came true. American women won the right to vote.

In 1979, her country honored her. Her image was shown on the one-dollar coin.

Chapter 4

Bethenia Owens-Adair

Pioneer Doctor

"You're just a puny girl. Bet you can't even budge that sack of flour," teased Bethenia's ten-year-old brother.

"Can too," 12-year-old Bethenia retorted. "Bet I can carry all four of them."

Flem snorted. "Sure you can."

"I'll show you," said Bethenia. "Help me get two of them on my shoulders."

Flem lifted two of the heavy sacks up on his sister's shoulders. She staggered under the weight. Then she squatted down to lift the other two. She slid one under each arm. "See," she panted.

Flem was determined not to show his admiration for her. "You couldn't have done it if I hadn't helped you."

"So? I did it, didn't I?" said Bethenia. "I'm just as good as any old boy. I can do anything you can do."

Bethenia could do just about anything Flem could do. She was small for her age, much smaller than Flem. But she could keep up with him. She could pitch hay, milk cows, and plant potatoes and beans.

Nine years before in 1843, the Owens family had moved from Missouri to Oregon in a Conestoga wagon. They settled on the Clatsop plain. It was at the mouth of the Columbia River.

Tom Owens had cleared the land for farming. He built a large, sturdy house for his growing family.

Bethenia loved their farm. She was never lonely with so many sisters and brothers. In addition to Flem, there was Diane, two years older than Bethenia. Josiah was eight. Mary was six. And there were babies who seemed to come along about every two years.

Everything was wonderful. That is until the day Papa came home from town and announced, "There's going to be a summer school. It starts next week. The young schoolteacher is going to stay with us."

"Oh, no," groaned Bethenia. "I don't want to go to school. Not in the summer." She tugged on Papa's arm. "Besides, you need me on the farm."

Papa smiled. "Flem will help me. Diane will help your mother. But you, Josiah, and Mary are going to school."

Mr. Beaufort, the handsome young teacher, moved into their house. Bethenia stopped complaining. She wouldn't have missed a day of school for anything. Bethenia was in love.

It was not easy to start an education at the age of 12. Letters and numbers were difficult to master. And learning to write seemed impossible.

But because Bethenia tried so hard, Mr. Beaufort gave her extra help.

"She has a lot of determination," Mr. Beaufort told her parents. "She can go far if she has an education."

Sarah Owens shook her head sadly. "Not much chance of that," she said. "I'd be proud to see all my children get educated. But there aren't any schools around."

Because of her love for her teacher, Bethenia began to take an interest in her appearance. She made sure her dresses were always clean and neat. Every night before she went to bed, she brushed her long hair until it shone. But Mr. Beaufort continued thinking of her as a little girl and his pupil.

Bethenia started attracting young boys in the area. There was John Adair, a handsome, polite young lad from Kentucky. Le Grand Hill was tall and strong. But he would rather hunt and fish than anything. Then there was John Hobson. He began showering his attention on Diane.

All too soon summer was over. Mr. Beaufort had to leave for another teaching job. Bethenia thought her heart would surely break when she said good-bye to him.

But Mr. Beaufort still treated Bethenia like a small child. Before he left, he picked her up, held her in his arms for a moment, and kissed her. When he left, Bethenia ran into the barn and sobbed herself to sleep.

A year later, Tom Owens sold his farm on the Clatsop plain. He moved his family south to the small village of Roseburg.

Diane stayed behind and married John Hobson. Le Grand Hill and his family moved south also.

The following spring, at the age of 14, Bethenia married Le Grand. Within a short time, it was apparent that her husband was not a good provider. And after their son George was born two years later, a streak of meanness began to show.

Little George was a sickly baby. His father had no patience with him. Le Grand seldom worked. The more he stayed around the house, the more difficult Bethenia's life became. They argued over his harsh treatment of the child.

By the time George was two, Bethenia could not live with Le Grand any longer. She went back home and filed for divorce. She changed her name back to Owens.

Sarah Owens was a great comfort to her daughter. "You're only 18 years old, Bethenia. Life is not over. You must forget about the past and start over again."

"But how?" Bethenia cried. "How can I support myself? I can barely read and write."

Suddenly she had an idea. "I want to go to school," she told her parents.

"School!" Tom Owens exclaimed. "You're a grown woman with a child."

Sarah intervened. "And what of it? I'll take care of George. Bethenia has the courage to go to school with children. She knows she may be teased. And I'm behind her all the way."

Bethenia *was* teased. But her courage kept her going. At the end of the first four-month term, she had completed the third reader. She was doing better than average in arithmetic, geography, and spelling.

But her father insisted she come home. All the hard work was putting a strain on her.

In 1860, Bethenia went to Washington to visit a friend. She

spent the winter there and attended a nearby school. Later, she spent some time with her sister Diane and her husband, John, in Astoria. While there, she received more schooling.

At the supper table one evening, Bethenia asked John, "Would you think I was foolish if I started a little summer school?"

John replied, "It sounds like a fine idea. You contact the folks around here. See how many pupils you can get. I'll see if I can find a building you can use."

Bethenia opened her school in a church with 16 pupils. She received two dollars each for three months.

Some of Bethenia's students were more advanced in their studies than she was. However, they didn't know. Every night, Bethenia took their books home. With some tutoring from John, she was able to stay ahead of her class.

Over the years, Bethenia held many jobs. These included owning a hat store, taking more teaching positions, washing and ironing clothes, and nursing sick people.

It was the nursing that gave her the most satisfaction. More and more, she thought about studying medicine.

She knew her family would be opposed to the idea. "Maybe I should be content simply nursing sick folks," she told herself.

But one night, she was asked to help with a small child suffering from a bladder infection. An old doctor came to see the little girl. He attempted to use a **catheter.** His hand slipped, and the child was badly cut. Bethenia took the instrument from his hand and inserted it easily. The child's screams stopped.

The old doctor was angry. "How dare you?" he lashed out at Bethenia. "You are not a doctor."

Bethenia answered calmly, "No, I am not. But I shall be."

The next day, Bethenia called on her friend Dr. Hamilton. She told him of her dream to study medicine. He let her borrow some medical books, including *Gray's Anatomy.*

"It won't be easy," he said. "Most people have the fool notion that only men should be doctors. Finding a school will be hard enough."

"Do you know of any schools that will take women?" she asked.

"I'd try Philadelphia. I believe they take women at the Philadelphia Eclectic School of Medicine."

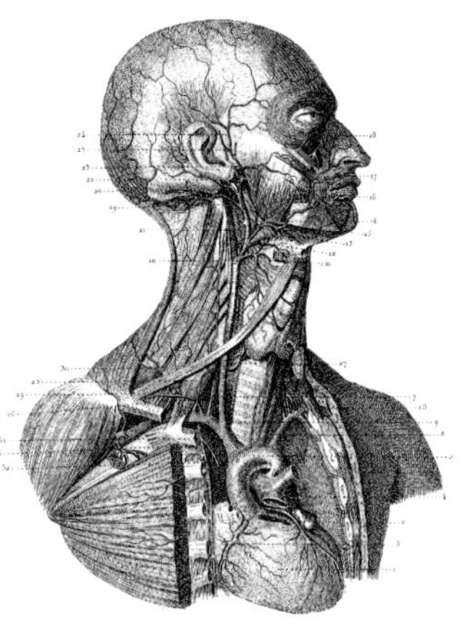

For a year, Bethenia secretly studied *Gray's Anatomy* and other medical books. Then she was off to Philadelphia.

George was away at school, so he was no problem. But he was upset over his mother's plan to become a doctor.

"How can you disgrace your family this way?" he cried. "Especially since I am going into medicine myself." Bethenia tried hard not to let it bother her.

She was excited when she finally arrived in Philadelphia. She contacted the man Dr. Hamilton had told her about.

"I'm interested in enrolling in the Philadelphia Eclectic School of Medicine," she told the doctor. "But I'm not sure what kind of school it is."

"It is the practice of using nature's plants and drugs in healing. The school does not teach surgery."

Bethenia was disappointed. But at least it was a start.

She was accepted at the school. She also found a doctor who taught classes in medicine. She was the only woman in his class. She attended lectures and clinics at the famous Blockley Hospital. She saw **autopsies** performed by great surgeons.

At the end of the year, she received her diploma. Then she went to New York to study a new method of electric healing baths.

Not long after she had arrived back home, a group of doctors prepared to do an autopsy. Dr. Palmer was there. He was the doctor who had injured the little girl. Sarcastically, he suggested, "Maybe we should send for the new 'she doctor.' She can show us how skillful she is."

The other doctors agreed.

Bethenia received the written invitation. She suspected at once that they did not mean it. But she was not about to back down.

When she arrived, she opened the door. Bethenia was met by loud laughter from the crowd who had come to watch. She saw surprise as well as scorn in the faces of the doctors.

They didn't expect me to come, she thought.

She squared her shoulders and said, "Thank you for your invitation, fellow physicians. I am honored."

Old Dr. Palmer sputtered, "You can't be serious. You would disgrace yourself by attending a male autopsy?"

"I do not consider practicing my profession disgraceful," Bethenia retorted. "And furthermore, I would like to know why my attendance is different from yours at a female autopsy."

A young doctor interrupted. "We have invited Miss . . . uh . . . Dr. Owens. Perhaps she would be kind enough to perform the autopsy. Then she can give her professional opinion."

Bethenia did the autopsy. She reported her diagnosis. And then with head held high, she marched out of the building.

"She doctor! She doctor!" the crowd called after her.

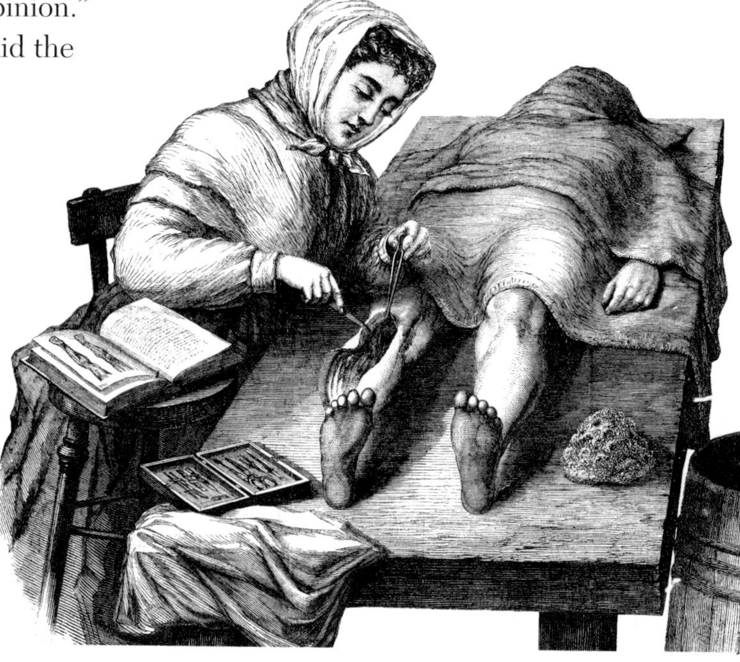

"Such scandalous behavior!" a woman yelled.

Bethenia was to face similar opposition for years to come. But it didn't stop her.

She moved to Portland and set up practice. The use of the medicated electric baths proved to be popular with her patients.

Bethenia was overjoyed to find that her son had changed his mind. "I was a narrow-minded fool," he admitted. "And I want you to know that I am very proud of you."

In 1878, Bethenia went back to school. She received a degree in medicine and added surgery to her list of skills.

At the age of 44, Bethenia married John Adair, a man she had known in her childhood.

Until October 1905, Bethenia practiced her profession proudly. She made house calls on horseback. Sometimes she traveled in raging snowstorms. She performed operations on kitchen tables. She saw many changes take place in the medical world.

A phrase that she had once stated was engraved on her headstone: "Only the enterprising and the brave are [driven] to become pioneers."

A most fitting **epitaph** for Bethenia Owens-Adair, pioneer doctor.

Chapter 5

Linda Richards

America's First Trained Nurse

Linda sat quietly beside her mother's bed. She tried not to show her fear. Only a few months ago, Papa had died. And now Mama was very ill.

Mrs. Richards smiled weakly at her daughter. "You're such a good little nurse," she said.

Nine-year-old Linda was much younger than her two sisters. But she took complete care of Mama. Linda could always coax Mama to swallow one more spoonful of broth. Her sisters could not. So the older girls did the cooking and cleaned the house.

Old Dr. Currier came from town every few days to see Mrs. Richards. He praised the small girl. "We will have your mother well in no time," he said. "With my medicine and your good care."

But all the medicine and nursing couldn't save Mama.

Dr. Currier tried to console Linda. "You took very good care of your mother, child," he said.

"But it wasn't enough," sobbed Linda. "I need to know more."

"Yes, you do," agreed the old doctor. "And as soon as you're old enough, I'll teach you."

After Mama died, 14-year-old Laura was sent to Boston to live with relatives. Elizabeth, aged 13, and Linda moved to Grandma and Grandpa Sinclair's farm.

Elizabeth helped Grandma in the house. Linda helped Grandpa in the fields and the barn. When an animal was sick or injured, Linda nursed it back to health.

She once stayed up all night with an old rooster. It had been badly hurt in a fight. In the morning, Dr. Currier stopped by. He found Linda asleep in the corner of the barn holding the rooster in her arms.

"You're not satisfied unless you're taking care of something," he laughed. "Even an old rooster."

It was Linda's thirteenth birthday. Dr. Currier announced, "Today, Miss Richards, you become my official helper."

Linda was thrilled.

In the next two years, she went with the doctor on many of his house calls. She learned how to set broken bones, stop bleeding, bandage wounds, and remove stitches.

After the old doctor's death, Linda spent several years teaching school. But she never gave up her desire to be a nurse.

Finally, she went to Boston.

Surely, she thought, I can find the training I need in one of the hospitals here.

But the doctors she talked to made fun of her when she asked if they would train her.

"Never!"

"Get married and raise babies. You'll get all the nursing you can handle."

The only job she could find was at Boston City Hospital as a ward maid. From sunup to sundown, she scrubbed floors, washed and

ironed sheets, and cooked meals. But she was not allowed to work with the patients. The doctors there were very rude when they found out she wanted to be a nurse.

"There's no place in a hospital for a woman nurse," they told her. "Leave the patients to the doctors."

Linda read everything she could about nursing. She learned about the Florence Nightingale nursing program in England.

Then one day, she saw a sign in a store window. A training program for nurses was starting at the New England Hospital for Women and Children.

Linda wasted no time. She was the first to enroll. One year later on September 1, 1873, she was the first to graduate. Melinda Ann Judson Richards was America's first trained nurse.

Job offers began to arrive. She accepted a position at the Bellevue Hospital Training School in New York. She was a night nursing superintendent. Linda worked with Sister Helen Bowden, who had trained in London.

Linda was shocked with the conditions at the hospital. Sister Helen said, "There are many changes that need to be made. Patients should be treated as human beings, not animals." Linda agreed.

At midnight, the heat in the hospital was turned off. There were no extra blankets. The lights were kept low. It was difficult even to see the patients while attending them. No written records of patients were kept.

Linda argued with the hospital board. "Our job is to save money," they said.

"And my job is to save lives," she responded.

The board finally gave in.

Linda had charts put at the foot of each bed. There the nurses could record the patient's vital signs and condition.

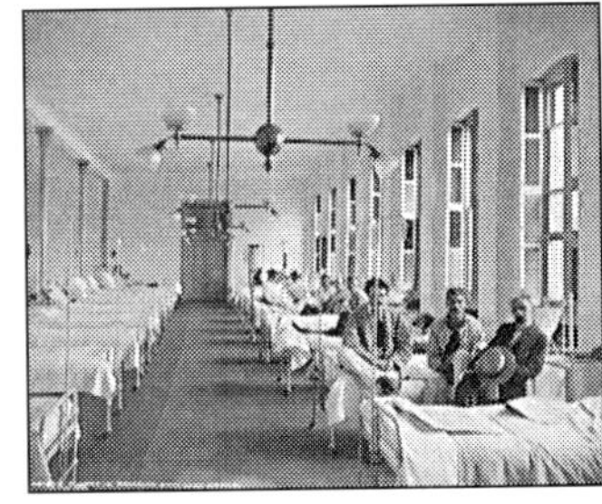

Linda's job was not only nursing. She also taught the students.

She suggested that nurses wear uniforms. One of her students designed a blue and white striped dress with a white apron and a white cap. Other hospitals soon followed this practice.

From Bellevue, Linda moved on to Massachusetts General Hospital to direct their nursing program. Little by little, doctors gave in to the idea of trained nurses in hospitals. Some of them even offered to help with the programs.

Though satisfied with the progress being made, Linda wanted to learn more about nursing. For years, she had dreamed of someday meeting the famous Florence Nightingale.

In April 1877, her dream came true. Linda had requested to visit Nightingale Training School in London. And she received an invitation!

Linda was very impressed with Florence Nightingale. During her stay in London, they became good friends. She discovered that many of England's methods of nursing were superior to America's.

Linda spent several months at the Nightingale Training School at St. Thomas's Hospital. Then she went to Paris. She visited training schools there.

Florence Nightingale

Finally, she was ready to sail back to America. She was anxious to pass on all she had learned.

At home, a new project was waiting for Linda. Dr. Cowles, the director of Boston City Hospital, wanted her to help with a nurses' training school.

Linda remembered the dislike she had met when she was a ward maid there. So she was a little hesitant. But she decided that if Dr. Cowles had faith in her it was worth a try.

Linda started a two-year training plan. She used many of the methods she had learned in England. She especially wanted nurses to be trained for the operating room.

The doctors at Boston City refused to be a part of the program. So Linda brought in nurses from other hospitals to help her teach the class.

In time, many of the doctors were won over. They began to see how helpful the program could be. Some of them actually offered to teach the students.

Linda heard that a hospital in Japan wanted to start a nursing program. She applied for the position and was accepted. It was at a mission hospital in Kyoto.

She arrived there in December 1885. She studied the Japanese language until she could speak with the students. Having two American mission doctors at the hospital helped.

Linda Richards

In the five years that Linda was in Japan, she learned a lot about the customs. One was that Japanese men did not take orders from women. When a male patient refused medicine from a student nurse, Linda solved the problem. She told him, "The doctor told her to give you the medicine. It is *his* order."

The man took the medicine.

❈ ❈ ❈

Back in America, Linda entered the Philadelphia Visiting Nurses Society. These nurses went into the homes of poor people who needed nursing. Linda enjoyed working with them. She taught them hygiene and good eating habits.

Her next job was directing nurses at a mental hospital in Taunton, Massachusetts. She stressed the importance of kindness in dealing with the patients. This was especially important for those who were confused and frightened. She also started a class to teach the mentally ill to work with their hands to make small items.

Linda Richards

Linda was 32 years old when she graduated from nurses' training. She was 70 when illness and exhaustion forced her to retire. She had spent nearly 40 years taking care of sick people and teaching others to do the same. She was responsible for many changes in the field of nursing.

In 1928, nurses at the New England Hospital for Women and Children heard that Linda was in a nursing home. They insisted that she be moved to the hospital.

On April 16, 1930, Melinda Ann Richards died at the hospital where 57 years before she had graduated as the first American-trained nurse.

Chapter 6

Marian Anderson

African American Singer

Marian Anderson

Arturo Toscannini was a famous orchestra conductor. He once said that Marian Anderson had a voice that comes "once in a hundred years."

Marian thrilled audiences for over 50 years with her rich **contralto** voice. She especially loved to sing **spirituals.** She chose ones that had been handed down from the days of slavery.

In 1908, Marian was six years old. Mr. Robinson was the choir leader in her church. He was surprised by Marian's rich voice. It was very good for a girl so young.

"I want you to take this music home. Practice it, Marian," he said. "I would like you to sing it next Sunday with your friend, Viola Johnson." It would be the first time Marian would sing in public.

The song was "Dear to the Heart of the Shepherd." Marian would sing this song for many years to come.

Viola's voice was high. Marian's was deep and mellow. And Marian's voice had great volume. She often drowned out Viola when they practiced.

"Not so loud," Viola complained several times.

"I'm sorry," Marian apologized.

After church services that Sunday, people came up to Marian's father. They said, "What a beautiful voice your little girl has."

"She sings like an angel."

“You must be very proud of her.”

John Anderson was proud of all three daughters—Marian and her younger sisters, Alice and Ethyl.

Mr. Anderson worked hard to support his family. He delivered coal to homes in Philadelphia in the winter. And in the summer, he delivered ice.

As a child, Marian dreamed of taking music lessons. But her parents could not afford it. She taught herself to play simple tunes on an old piano. But it bothered her. She knew she was not playing properly.

One day, Marian saw a violin in the window of a **pawnshop.** More that anything in the world she wanted that violin. Shyly, she went into the shop.

“How much is the violin?” she asked the **pawnbroker.**

“Three dollars and ninety-five cents,” the man answered. “It’s a fine violin. As good as any **Stradivarius.”**

Marian didn’t know what a Stradivarius was. But it sounded good. And she wanted that violin.

For weeks, she scrubbed neighbors’ porches. Each time, Marian earned five cents.

Finally, Marian proudly walked home carrying the violin. She had earned the money all by herself!

Marian began to play. But the strings snapped one by one as the bow touched them. Her father replaced them. But they would not stay tuned. Then the bridge broke and fell out.

The violin was very old and of poor quality. The instrument finally fell apart. So did Marian’s dream of becoming a famous concert violinist.

In 1912, John Anderson suffered a head injury while working. He died a short time later.

Mrs. Anderson had to do laundry and housework for others. She used the money she earned to feed and clothe her family.

Marian continued singing in her church. People all over town heard about the young black girl with the “voice like a nightingale.”

She received offers to sing at parties and other functions. Sometimes Marian earned as much as five dollars a performance.

Proudly, Marian would hand her mother the money she earned. Mrs. Anderson was a very devout woman. She would say, "This money comes from the Lord, Marian. It is His doing. Not just yours."

Marian agreed. She knew that her voice was a gift from God. And she intended to make the most of it. She would take music lessons.

Marian knew of a famous music school. It was in uptown Philadelphia. It had a good name. She arrived with high hopes and took her place in the long line.

Marian's turn finally came. The young girl handing out the applications glared at the young singer. She said coldly, "What do you want?"

"I want to fill out an application to enroll—"

Before Marian could finish, the young lady snapped, "We don't take coloreds."

Marian was more surprised than hurt. It was her first real experience with racial prejudice.

Marian had always lived in neighborhoods where Negroes and white people got along well. She attended schools with children of all races.

Marian was not a person to anger easily. Neither was her mother. Mrs. Anderson told her daughter, "There will be another way for you to get the help you need. Just have faith in the Lord."

Marian Anderson

Marian did have faith. And the congregation of the Union Baptist Church had faith in Marian. They gave a concert. The money from the ticket sales went to pay for a music teacher for Marian.

The teacher was Mary Patterson. She taught Marian everything she could.

One day, Mary said, "There's someone I would like you to meet. His name is Giuseppi Boghetti."

Marian had heard of the famous voice teacher.

Ms. Patterson took Marian to his studio. But the music teacher was very rude. "I have all the students I can handle. I absolutely will not take any more," he said.

"Please. Just listen to her sing," Ms. Patterson pleaded. "Please."

He gave in. He listened until Marian's last note of "Deep River" faded away. Mr. Boghetti gave a big sigh. He said, "I will make room for you right away. In two years you will be able to sing for anyone. Anywhere."

Mr. Boghetti was a very strict teacher. But Marian learned a lot from him. He taught her to breathe correctly and make the most of her voice. Marian worked hard.

Marian learned to sing songs by Schubert, Brahms, and Schumann. Until then, she had sung mostly spirituals and hymns. She learned to sing in German, Italian, and French.

Marian entered a singing contest shortly after she finished high school. She won over 300 other singers.

Marian Anderson

She had become an outstanding singer. But often Marian was not asked to perform in the large theaters. It seemed that the American people had a hard time admitting that a Negro could be so talented.

A musician friend suggested that Marian go to Europe to study and perform. She did. And she was a huge success! She was in demand everywhere.

Marian was overjoyed with the way she was treated abroad. But she missed her own country and family.

Marian Anderson was known all over the world by the time she got back to the United States. But she still faced prejudice. At times, hotels refused to give Marian a room. Or restaurants would not serve her. And she had to ride in the **Jim Crow** car when traveling by train.

But in the spring of 1939, Marian faced the greatest racial prejudice of her life. She was to give a concert in Washington, D.C. Her agent planned to rent Constitution Hall. The building was owned by the Daughters of the American Revolution (DAR).

Marian was refused the use of the hall because she was a Negro. The DAR did not want a black person to sing there.

When Marian read about it, she was sad and ashamed. But she was not ashamed of being a Negro. She was ashamed that there were people who condemned her for being a Negro.

Marian was contacted by news reporters. But she would not say a thing against the DAR. It was not Marian Anderson's way.

Many people were very angry. How could such a gifted person be treated so badly because of her race?

Eleanor Roosevelt and Marian Anderson

The first lady at the time was Eleanor Roosevelt. She was so angry that she immediately resigned from the DAR. She then arranged for the Lincoln Memorial to be the site of Marian Anderson's concert. Everyone was invited to attend—free of charge.

On Easter Sunday, April 9, 1939, Marian Anderson stood before the giant statue of Abraham Lincoln. The crowd reached 75,000 people.

Marian Anderson at Lincoln Memorial

Marian opened the program with the national anthem. Then the audience joined in as Marian sang "America." Marian sang a variety of music that day. When the applause and cheering finally died down, Marian spoke. Her voice trembled with emotion.

"I am overwhelmed. I just can't talk. I can't tell you what you have done for me today. I thank you from the bottom of my heart again and again."

In her autobiography, Marian Anderson wrote, "When I stood up to sing our National Anthem, I felt for a moment as though I were choking. For a desperate second, I thought that the words, well as I know them, would not come."

Marian Anderson (left) Eleanor Roosevelt (right)

She had never felt such emotion from a performance. And never had she been so accepted by an audience.

❋ ❋ ❋

In later years, a mural marking the event was painted in the Department of Interior Building. Marian attended the unveiling.

Marian did one day sing in Constitution Hall. But she felt no sense of triumph. It was simply another performance in another auditorium.

In 1943, Marian married Orpheus Fisher.

Marian received many honors in her lifetime. They came from other countries as well as the United States. She was the first black person to sing a major role in the Metropolitan Opera.

King George VI and Eleanor Roosevelt

She was the first African American to sing at the White House. President Roosevelt invited her to sing for England's King George VI when he visited in 1939.

In 1963, Marian sang during the March on Washington. Later, Dr. Martin Luther King Jr. gave his "I Have a Dream" speech.

Dr. Martin Luther King Jr.

Marian Anderson gave her last concert at New York's Carnegie Hall. She was over 60 years old. Her voice was still rich and strong.

After the concert, she retired. Marian and her husband had built a beautiful home in Connecticut years before. They called it "Marianna Farm."

There, Marian spent her time doing the things she had always been too busy for. Cooking, sewing, gardening, and caring for her pets. But most of all, she played the piano and sang the songs that had thrilled audiences all over the world.

In 1986, her husband died. Their home was sold a few years later.

When Marian Anderson turned 90, she moved to Portland, Oregon. She lived with her nephew, conductor James DePriest, and his wife.

Miss Anderson died April 8, 1993.

Chapter 7

Margaret Bourke-White

Photographer of Life

Five-year-old Margaret sat on the top step. She watched an insect crawl across the porch. "Don't step on it, Papa," she cried.

Mr. White knelt down beside his daughter. "It's a May beetle, Margaret," he said. "They hatch underground in the roots of plants."

Of course, Margaret already knew this. She and her older sister, Ruth, had inherited their interest in nature from their parents.

The White family lived in Bound Brook, New Jersey. Their house sat in a grove of trees. There were meadows and rolling hills nearby.

Margaret and Ruth knew the names of everything—every wildflower that grew, every insect that crawled or flew, and every small animal that lived in the burrows and trees. Margaret's favorite times were the nature walks with her father.

Margaret would sit for hours to watch a **chrysalis** split open. She would watch as the wet, shapeless mass changed into a beautiful butterfly.

She once found a baby robin that had fallen from its nest. She worried about how to save that tiny chick. It wouldn't eat anything. Sadly, Margaret sat on the ground, put the robin on her lap, and prayed that it wouldn't die. Suddenly, an adult robin lit beside the

baby bird. Its mouth was full of mushy worm. Then the adult began to feed the baby robin.

Margaret was thrilled. But she sat stone still and watched the miracle. After a few days, the **fledgling** flew away with its parents.

Margaret was very interested in snakes. Her father taught her and her sister how to tell a harmless snake from a poisonous one. He showed them how to pick up a snake. Margaret's father even gave her a boa constrictor for a pet.

The house was often filled with snakes, toads, and jars of insects. An old puff adder made its home with the family. It would curl up on Mrs. White's lap while she sat before the fireplace reading. Understandably, many people were a little afraid to visit the Whites.

Margaret's interest in snakes was so great that she planned to become a herpetologist, an expert on snakes. "I'll travel all over the world searching for rare species. I'll do all the things that women never do," she stated.

Margaret could handle snakes the way most children handled puppies and kittens. But she had one fear. She was afraid of the dark. She would wake the family with her piercing screams in the middle of the night.

"There was something in my room," she would cry. "A monster."

Finally, Mrs. White solved the problem. On darkest nights, she would take Margaret outside and make her walk around the house all alone. She herself would walk around in the opposite direction.

Just as Margaret's fear would reach its peak, she would come face to face with her mother. They would throw themselves into each other's arms and break out laughing.

Little by little, Margaret overcame her fear of the dark. And she discovered that the night was full of interesting nature sounds. She actually learned to enjoy it.

Joseph White was patient and easygoing with his children. His wife, Minnie, was a strong disciplinarian. She believed in building character at an early age. She stressed the importance of tackling difficult problems over easy ones.

"The easy way is usually the wrong way," she said. "The right way is always hard."

Until she was 11 years old, Margaret's handwriting was very hard to read. For her birthday, Mrs. White gave her a diary with a note.

Dear Margaret,

If you will practice writing in this book every day or at least five days each week during vacations, and your handwriting shows improvement by Sept. 30, you may make out a list of surprises, one of which you would like as a reward.

Your loving mother

P.S. It would be a good plan to choose a sentence for each page and write it over and over until the page is filled.

Mrs. White's plan worked. Within a few years, Margaret had developed very good penmanship.

As a child, Margaret loved going to the factory where her father worked. She loved watching the machines.

Her father once took her to a **foundry** that was making parts for some of his machines. Margaret was thrilled. She was fascinated by the sparks shooting through the air like fireworks.

"I have never heard of a girl being interested in machines and such," Margaret's mother complained. "Why can't she stick to sewing and cooking like other girls?"

Mr. White only smiled. "But she does like cooking and sewing, Mother. There's nothing wrong with being interested in other things too."

Margaret was interested in a great many things. However, photography was not one of them. This did not interest her until much later.

When Margaret was 14, she entered a school writing competition and won. Margaret had a few close friends. But she was not overly popular in high school. Part of the reason may have been that she was not allowed to play cards, wear makeup, chew gum, or do many things that her classmates did.

She participated in swimming, basketball, and hockey. One year, Margaret was elected president of her class. She was also an editor of the high school senior class book.

Margaret was 17 when she graduated from high school.

In the fall of 1921, Margaret entered Teachers College at Columbia University. She still planned to study snakes. Some of her subjects were French, biology, and drawing.

She also took a photography class from Clarence H. White at his School of Photography. Mr. White was known for his photographs that looked like paintings. Many of them hung in museums.

Mr. White was a great influence on Margaret. After she had become a successful photographer, she said, "The seed was planted with that course."

That summer, Margaret took a job teaching photography at a children's camp. She taught the campers to take and develop pictures. She also taught them all she could about nature.

Margaret took a number of photos of the camp and nearby woods and lake. The camp directors saw the photos. They offered to pay her for 200 prints to be used on postcards.

The postcards sold quickly to visiting parents. The directors ordered 500 more. Margaret also sold several hundred of her postcards in gift shops in town.

In her diary, Margaret wrote, "I am so proud of myself. I feel as if I can make my living anywhere."

In September 1926, Margaret moved to upstate New York and attended Cornell University. She began taking pictures of buildings on the campus. Many of these were printed in the *Cornell Alumni News* for five dollars each.

More and more, Margaret was seeing her future in photography. This surprised her. She had always thought taking pictures was a hobby. Something to do for fun. Not a way to make a living!

Margaret Bourke-White

Margaret did get a degree in herpetology. But she turned down a job offer from the Museum of Natural History in New York. Instead, she moved to Cleveland, Ohio.

Photo by Margaret Bourke-White

Margaret rented a one-room apartment. She added her mother's maiden name to her own and opened the first Margaret Bourke-White Studio. She used the kitchen area for the darkroom and the bathtub for washing her prints.

Margaret continued taking architectural photographs, which were published in magazines. But she still found as much excitement in machinery and industry as she had when her father took her to his factory.

She saw beauty and form in smokestacks, bridge arches, steel towers, cranes, and steel mill furnaces. A photograph she took of a 200-ton ladle at the Otis Steel Company in 1928 was an award winner.

Margaret once said, "**Dynamos** are more beautiful than pearls."

In 1929, she went to work for publisher Henry Luce. He had started a new magazine called *Fortune.* Margaret was staff photographer and assistant editor.

When Henry Luce started *Life* magazine in 1936, Margaret was asked to join the staff. Her pictures of the construction of Fort Peck Dam in Montana were on the cover of the first issue.

Erskine Caldwell and Margaret Bourke-White

In 1937, she collaborated on the book *You Have Seen Their Faces* with author Erskine Caldwell. Later they married. But, unfortunately, that marriage ended in divorce.

In a field usually only for men, Margaret Bourke-White became one of the most famous photographers in the world. As she had long ago predicted, she traveled all over the world "doing things that women never do."

And she did them well.

The lesson she learned from her mother stayed with her all her life. "The easy way is usually the wrong way," Mrs. White had said. "The right way is always hard."

Right or not, Margaret did most things the hard way.

It was nothing for her to crawl along a **catwalk** in a factory to get just the right shot. She often climbed into an overhead crane or balanced herself atop a tottering ladder.

As *Life*'s aerial photographer, she once dangled by a cable from a helicopter. From this position, she took a picture of a flock of snow geese in flight.

Nothing was too difficult for Margaret Bourke-White. At least not until she was working in Korea in the early 1950s.

Margaret began to notice a stiffening in her joints. Within a few months, her hands began to tremble and her speech became slurred.

Margaret had Parkinson's disease, an incurable, crippling disease. She underwent two operations which gave her some relief for a while. She tried all kinds of exercises and therapy.

Margaret spent hours dipping towels in water. Then she wrung them out. She lifted weights and did knee bends. She never gave in to her illness.

In an interview, she said, "If you banish fear, nothing terribly bad can happen to you."

Margaret had banished fear many times in her life. From the childhood fear of the dark to the fear of her disease. She made appearances before other people with the illness. She encouraged them all she could.

Toward the end of her life, Margaret became paralyzed and was confined to a wheelchair. She lost her ability to speak.

In August 1971, Margaret Bourke-White died. But the legacy she left the world will live forever.

Photo by Margaret Bourke-White

Chapter 8

Jackie Cochran

First Lady of Aviation

Jackie Cochran once said, "Pity the man or woman who doesn't have the chance to love the way I loved flying."

For 40 years, she satisfied that love. When Jackie died in 1980 at the age of 69, she held more records in aviation for speed, altitude, and distance than any other flyer—man or woman.

At the age of 25, Jackie married Floyd Odlum. He was one of the ten richest men in the world. She herself became a millionaire from the cosmetic business she founded in 1935.

She had come a long way from Sawdust Road, where she'd spent her childhood.

Sawdust Road was any poor part of a town. It was where the sawmill workers lived. The one-room shacks had no electricity or water. Some didn't even have windows. Jackie's Sawdust Road was in southern Florida.

When she was about six years old, she overheard a conversation between Mama and a neighbor.

"Reckon her folks will ever come back for her?" the neighbor asked.

Mama answered, "Don't reckon. It ain't easy. But I promised I'd bring her up. She's a burden I have to bear."

Jackie sat motionless behind the shed where she was hiding. She could hardly contain the joy she felt. She wasn't one of them!

Somehow, even at that early age, she felt different from her family. She felt as though she didn't belong.

The two boys, Henry and Joe, and the two girls, Mamie and Myrtle, were several years older than Jackie.

Mama and the girls were unclean and lazy. Sometimes they'd go weeks without bathing or without even combing their hair.

Jackie had a thing about being clean, even when she was very small. Her family had no hot water. So every morning, she would fill a tub with cold water and scrub herself.

"Mighty high and mighty, ain't she?" her foster sisters would sneer.

"At least, I don't stink," Jackie would snap back.

Papa and the boys were dirty too. And they chewed tobacco and spit on the floor.

In the summer, the odor in the cabin was terrible. Whenever she could, Jackie slept outside. It was better than sleeping on the floor anyway.

Jackie never owned a pair of shoes until she was eight years old. Most of the time she was hungry and cold.

One day, she was in the woods looking for something to eat. She saw a farmer cooking a pan of sweet potatoes over an open fire. Jackie knew they were hog food. But the smell of those sweet potatoes was heavenly. Her stomach lurched just thinking how good they would taste.

Then, wonder of wonders, the farmer turned and went into his house. In a flash, Jackie ran to the pan and scooped out two large, hot sweet potatoes. She darted into the woods and gulped them down. Her mouth burned with every bite. It was the first meal she'd had in two days.

One of the biggest thrills of Jackie's childhood was when a circus came to town. The thrill was more than the elephants, the clowns, and the bearded lady. It was the chance to escape. Jackie made up her mind that when the circus left, she would leave with it.

No more Sawdust Road for Jackie Cochran. She was leaving it all behind.

She'd show the circus people what a good worker she was. All day, she hauled water for the elephants. At the end of the day, she felt as though her arms would fall off.

That night, she curled up on a pile of straw. She knew the circus would leave early. And she wanted to be up and ready. But when the sun woke her, the circus was gone. Someone had covered her with a burlap sack.

Jackie blinked back tears. It would be a few more years before she would escape Sawdust Road. But someday—

Jackie's first attempt at an education failed. On the third day of school, the teacher tried to spank her. Jackie slapped the teacher. Then she bolted out the door and never went back.

The next year, Jackie heard there was a new teacher. She decided to give it another try.

Jackie loved Miss Boswick. If she had stayed at the school, Jackie would gladly have gone every day. But two years later, Miss Boswick left Sawdust Road. Jackie gave up learning.

When she was only eight, Jackie began doing housework and baby-sitting for people in the mill town. But her foster mother took all the money she earned.

Next Jackie went to work in a cotton mill. When she was ten, she was made supervisor over 15 other children.

A year later, Jackie went to live with a lady who owned a beauty salon. She cooked, cleaned, and cared for her children.

In time, the lady let Jackie help in the shop. She shampooed customers' hair. Finally, Jackie learned how to give permanents.

When she was less than 14, a salesman came into the salon. He was looking for someone to operate a new permanent wave machine in Montgomery, Alabama. Jackie jumped at the chance.

It was the beginning of her career in the cosmetic business.

One of her customers was a juvenile court judge. She took a liking to Jackie.

"You're a bright girl, Jackie," she said. "And you're clever with your hands. You should do something else with your life."

At first, Jackie just shrugged it off. But the lady was very persuasive. She talked Jackie into taking nurse's training.

Jackie had been poor for a long time. And soon she became dissatisfied with a nurse's life and wages. And it seemed that all of her nursing was in mill towns.

I might as well be back on Sawdust Road, she told herself.

Jackie gave up nursing.

When she was 20, Jackie went to work for a high-class hair stylist in New York City. As her list of wealthy customers grew, so did her bank account. Jackie Cochran was on her way up. She had left Sawdust Road behind her forever.

Through the sales of cosmetics, Jackie met a lot of interesting people. It was at a dinner party that she met her future husband, Floyd Odlum. She confided in him her dream to have her own cosmetic business and travel all over the country selling.

Jokingly, Floyd said, "Then you better get some wings." It was no joke to Jackie.

Not long afterward, Jackie began a three-week vacation. The first day, Jackie went to the Roosevelt Field Flying School. She asked an instructor, "I'd like to learn to fly a plane. How long will it take to get a license?"

The pilot was Husky Lewellyn. He answered, "About two months, maybe three."

"I don't have that much time," Jackie said impatiently. "I only have three weeks."

"I'm afraid that's not enough time," smiled the pilot. "No one can earn a license in three weeks."

Jackie answered, "I can."

Jackie began her first lesson. No sooner had the plane left the ground than Jackie's heart began beating wildly. It was not from fear but excitement. Never had she felt this way. Flying was in her blood. And it would be for the rest of her life.

In less than three weeks, Jackie had her license. She didn't know the difference between a biplane and a monoplane. She couldn't read a compass. But she had a license to fly!

In 1933, Jackie enrolled in a flying school in San Diego. She felt she needed more instruction. Jackie worried about the written tests she would have to take. She had so little education. Her writing and spelling were terrible.

The school let Jackie take the test orally. She passed the test with the highest possible rating. She got her commercial license.

Then Jackie heard about racing.

Jackie didn't win the first few races she entered. But it didn't discourage her. Jackie wanted to race. Nothing was going to stop her! Not even an unfair rule of the Bendix Cross-Country Race.

In 1935, Jackie tried to sign up for the Bendix Cross-Country Race. The people in charge said, "Sorry, this race is just for men."

Jackie was very angry. "Why?" she demanded.

The reason was ridiculous. In 1933, a female racer was killed when her plane crashed.

Did these people think the same thing would happen to every woman pilot? And what if it had happened to a man?

Jackie had an idea. She went to every man who was entered in the race. She asked them to sign a paper. It said that it was all right with them if she entered.

Amelia Earhart

It worked. But Jackie had engine trouble halfway through the race. She had to drop out. But a friend, Amelia Earhart, entered and came in fifth.

In 1937, Jackie won first place in the women's division of the Bendix Air Race and third place overall. In that year, she also won the Harmon Trophy as outstanding female pilot of the year.

She had set three major records.

- Women's national speed record.
- Women's world speed record.
- New speed record of 4 hours, 12 minutes, 27 seconds from New York to Miami.

Jackie Cochran

Eleanor Roosevelt

First Lady Eleanor Roosevelt made the presentation. During the years to come, Jackie won 14 more Harmon Trophies.

Jackie had many close calls over the years. Once the plane she was flying caught fire while she was at 12,000 feet. There was one thing Jackie feared. It was a fire in a plane. She radioed the nearest airport to have fire-fighting equipment ready.

The heat in the plane was intense. The smoke was so thick that Jackie could hardly see the landing field. There was no time even to put the flaps down.

Seconds before the plane hit the ground, Jackie jumped out. The dry grass along the runway caught fire. All of her clothes and her case of cosmetics burned in the plane. But Jackie did not have one small burn. She did suffer an injury though. She broke her toe.

Before World War II, America delivered flying equipment to England. Jackie was the first woman to fly a bomber across the Atlantic.

She had an idea. Jackie discussed her plan with President Franklin Roosevelt. He approved.

So with 25 women pilots, she organized the WASPs (Women's

WASPS

More than 1,000 women served in the Women's Air Force Service Pilots. Most had learned to fly before the war. They had the important role of flying airplanes between military bases. They also delivered cargo. And they tested new planes. Their work freed up men to fly in combat.

Air Force Service Pilots). In 1945, Jackie received the Distinguished Service Medal for founding and directing the program.

Colonel Chuck Yeager

Colonel Chuck Yeager was the first male pilot to fly faster than the speed of sound. Jackie Cochran was the first female pilot to do the same.

Jackie was still setting records when she was nearly 60 years old.

How right Chuck Yeager was when he said, "Sometimes even Jackie Cochran couldn't believe what she had accomplished."

Jackie Cochran

Glossary

astronomer	person who studies the skies, planets, stars, etc.
autopsy	examination of a body after death to determine the cause of death
catheter	tube that is inserted into the body to drain fluids or infection
catwalk	narrow walkway usually suspended above machinery or action below
chronometer	timepiece that is designed to keep time with great accuracy
chrysalis	insect stage that happens between the larva and the butterfly; the cocoon
contralto	voice range lower than soprano (highest) and higher than tenor
dynamo	powerful generator
eclipse	total or partial obstruction of one celestial body by another
epitaph	inscription on a tombstone; a brief statement about a person's life
fledgling	baby bird that is still dependent on its parents
foundry	place where metal is melted and poured into molds
grit	firmness of mind and spirit; courage in the face of hardship or danger

Jim Crow	laws of the late 19th and early 20th centuries that made segregation legal
nebula	large body of gas and dust in space
overseer	manager; person who took care of running a plantation and managed the slaves
pawnbroker	person who owns a pawnshop
pawnshop	place where people can get a loan by letting the owner keep some property until the loan is paid back
sextant	instrument that measures distance for navigation using the altitude of stars, planets, etc.
spiritual	emotionally religious song developed by Southern blacks
Stradivarius	violin of the highest quality made by Antonio Stradivari during the 17th and 18th centuries; very valuable
temperance	abstinence (staying away) from alcoholic beverages

Index